OFFICIALLY
WITHDRAWN

SERVING IN THE MARINE CORPS

Alix Wood

Powe

New

Published in 2014 by Rosen Publishing
29 East 21st Street, New York, NY 10010

Editor for Alix Wood Books: Eloise Macgregor
Designer: Alix Wood
Researcher: Kevin Wood
Military Consultant: Group Captain MF Baker MA RAF (Retd)
Educational Consultant: Amanda Baker BEd (Hons) PGCDL

Photo Credits: Cover, 1, 4, 5 top and bottom, 6, 7, 8, 9, 10, 11, 12, 13, 14, 15,
16, 17, 18, 19, 20, 21 top and middle, 22, 23, 24, 25, 26, 27, 28, 29, 31 ©
Defenseimagery.mil; 21 bottom © Shutterstock; 5 middle © US Government

Library of Congress Cataloging-in-Publication Data

Wood, Alix.
 Serving in the Marine Corps / by Alix Wood.
     pages cm. — (Protecting our country)
Includes index.
  ISBN 978-1-4777-1296-2 (library binding) — ISBN 978-1-4777-1398-3 (pbk.) —
ISBN 978-1-4777-1399-0 (6-pack)
1. United States. Marine Corps—Juvenile literature. 2. Marines—United States—
Juvenile literature. I. Title.
VE23.W658 2014
359.9'60973—dc23
                                    2013002102

Manufactured in the United States of America

CPSIA Compliance Information: Batch #S13PK3: For Further Information contact Rosen Publishing, New York, New York at 1-800-237-9932

Contents

What Do the Marines Do?

The armed services are made up of highly skilled and trained men and women who defend our country. The Marine Corps is an **expeditionary** task force that can attack from the air, land, and sea.

The Marine Corps is the smallest branch of the military, with around 203,000 on active duty. The Marine Corps often works closely with the US Navy, but it is a separate force.

Marines in blue dress uniform

FACT FILE

The US Navy's elite force, the Navy SEALs, is a small unit used for special missions. Marines are used for special missions, too. However, the Marine Corps is a complete service, so its cooks, infantry, and mechanics are all trained marines.

The Marine Corps motto is "*Semper fidelis,*" which means always faithful. "Semper Fidelis" is also the title of the official march of the Marine Corps.

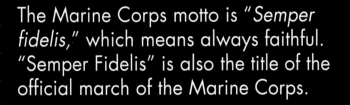

Every marine is a trained rifleman. A marine's skills are retested each year. All marines need to be capable of handling a weapon if necessary. Even marines whose main job never involves using firearms are trained to use a rifle. This means that any marine can do jobs like go on patrol or escort a **convoy**. Every marine learns and recites the Rifleman's Creed in training.

A marine uses the scope on his rifle to scan the area for enemy during a security patrol in Afghanistan.

Training

To become a marine, a soldier has to endure 13 weeks of training. Drill instructors train the **recruits**. They spend a lot of time yelling instructions and correcting any little mistake. They need to be tough to turn recruits into good soldiers.

An average day begins before sunrise. A bugle call called "reveille" is sounded. Recruits start physical training before breakfast. They have classes, drill, or martial arts between breakfast and lunch. Training continues until the evening meal. Recruits can then shower, clean their weapons, and tidy up their barracks. They have one hour off to write letters, work out, or do laundry. Lights-out is between 8:00 and 10:00 p.m., depending on the next day's activities.

A drill instructor

Marines training in the hot sun.

The first order a new recruit receives is "get off of my bus right now." The second order is "get on my yellow footprints right now." Thousands of marines have stood on these formation footprints at boot camp and thousands more will in years to come.

A Marine Corps cadence is a chant led by a loud drill instructor and repeated by a group of marching marines. Most marines first experience this at boot camp. Cadences motivate marines, keeping them all in step and breathing together at the right time.

You can keep your Army khaki,
You can keep your Navy blue,
I have the World's best fighting man,
To introduce to you.
His uniform is different,
The best you've ever seen,
The Germans called him "Devil Dog"
His real name is "Marine."

New male recruits have their hair clipped short. Women must keep their hair tied back if it is longer than collar length. There are strict rules about length of sideburns and types of mustaches, too.

Marine Traditions

The Marine Corps has many customs. They are important because they remind marines of their **heritage** and tradition. They also make members feel part of the team, which creates a strong bond of loyalty between them.

One of their most famous customs is the Marine Corps' birthday. Since 1921, it has been celebrated each year on November 10, the date in 1775 when the Marine Corps was created. It is celebrated even in combat zones. A section from the Marine Corps manual is usually read and a birthday message comes from the Commandant.

FACT FILE

Marines use many navy terms around the barracks:
Starboard: Right
Port: Left
Deck: Floor
Porthole: Window
Bulkhead: Wall
Galley: Kitchen
Mess: Dining area
Head: Restroom
Scuttlebutt: Water fountain

The cake is cut by the commanding **officer** and then the first and second slices are presented to the oldest and youngest marines present.

Marine leaders look out for their men. They make sure that they are comfortably clothed, housed, and justly treated. For example, a Marine Corps officer in the field gets into in the mess line after all the **enlisted** men to make sure all the men get fed first.

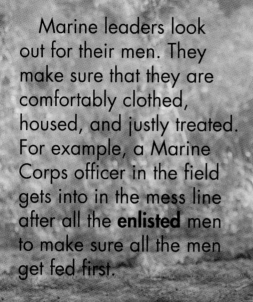

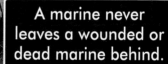

A marine never leaves a wounded or dead marine behind.

The Marine Corps' Silent Drill Platoon is a 24-man rifle platoon, also called the Marching Twenty-Four. It performs silent exhibition drills. **Bayoneted** rifles fly from marine to marine with discipline, precision, and skill. Wearing their crisp dress blue uniforms, not a single word is spoken during the drill.

9

Riflemen

Every marine is first and foremost a rifleman. As marines are often the first troops into an area, it is important that they can all defend themselves and protect others, no matter what their specialty is.

Marines can also specialize to be riflemen. They are trained to use rifles and **grenade** launchers, as well as automatic rifles and rockets. Riflemen often work in fire teams of four, along with a team leader who is also the grenadier, an automatic rifleman, and an assistant who carries extra **ammunition**.

A marine infantryman helps escort a supply vehicle.

From 500 yards (457 m), every marine is accurate with a rifle. Attach the bayonet, and the weapon becomes just as effective in close combat situations. The bayonet can also be used as a marine's multi-purpose fighting knife. Every marine receives bayonet training during martial arts training and on the bayonet assault course during recruit training.

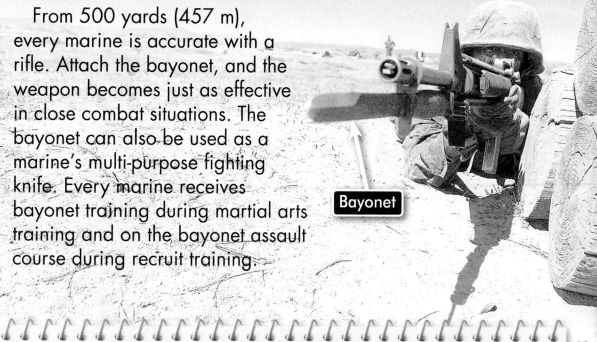

Bayonet

 ## FACT FILE

An excerpt from the Rifleman's Creed

This is my rifle. There are many like it, but this one is mine. My rifle is my best friend. It is my life. I must master it as I must master my life.

My rifle, without me, is useless. Without my rifle, I am useless. I must fire my rifle true. I must shoot straighter than my enemy who is trying to kill me. I must shoot him before he shoots me.

Unarmed Combat

Marines need to be able to fight even if they have no weapons available. They learn a mixture of different martial arts which develop their minds, their characters, and their physical abilities.

The motto of the Marine Corp's martial arts program is "one mind, any weapon." In other words, every marine is always armed, even without a weapon. He is armed with a combat mindset, the ability to assess and to act, and the knowledge that all marines can rely on one another.

Practicing martial arts at sea

Martial arts training

FACT FILE

Belts are awarded to show the level a marine has achieved. Because the belts are worn with the combat uniform, bright colors are avoided. The first level is a tan belt, then gray, green, brown, and black. There are six levels of black belts.

Marines learn different unarmed combat techniques to let them choose the best amount of force for a situation. For example, a marine facing a nonviolent but reluctant person can use a **restraint** technique. These cause no damage or pain to captives. A more aggressive person could be met with a choke, hold, or a strike. Lethal force can be used as a last resort.

Marine Convoys

Military vehicles often travel together in a convoy for protection. Convoys are often loaded with vital supplies and are slow-moving. They can be attacked in unstable areas, even if only to rob them of their supplies. Marines can be used to guard the convoys.

In 2006, around one third of all convoys in Iraq were attacked. Marines who guard convoys must be alert and organised. The head is the first vehicle in the convoy and carries the pacesetter. The pacesetter sets the speed needed to meet the schedule. The trail is the last vehicle and is responsible for discipline, breakdowns, straggling vehicles, and controlling things if there is an accident or incident.

Night convoys need to be kept small. Sometimes they must drive with no lights. Members need to go very slowly and stay close together.

Marines use many of the same vehicles as the army, like Humvees and Abrams tanks. They have some unique vehicles, too. The convoy of **amphibious** assault vehicles, or AAVs, to the left is on an exercise, in which marines practice what they would do in combat. These vehicles can operate on land or in the water.

Because of the dangers of convoy travel, unmanned convoy vehicles are being developed. A conversion kit can be fitted into new or old vehicles. The Marine Corps already flies unmanned **cargo** helicopters, too.

The Marine Corps uses helicopters and other aircraft to transport marines into an area and to fire on any enemy near its ground forces. Aircraft also transport supplies.

The Osprey has the speed of a plane and the hovering ability of a helicopter. It can be used for transporting troops or cargo, or for flying special forces operations. It stores compactly on board an aircraft carrier or assault ship. Its rotors can tilt vertically to hover and horizontally to power the aircraft along.

Rotors tilted forward

An Osprey can carry 24 combat troops.

FACT FILE

Aircraft can be used to provide covering fire when marines enter **hostile** areas. Door gunners use machine guns to provide suppressive fire when the helicopter has to land in a hostile area.

Marines learn how to rappel in their training. Rappelling is moving in a controlled way down a rope, from either a tall building or an aircraft. It can be dangerous. In a helicopter, the pilot must keep the helicopter steady. It is important to check all the equipment, and the ground below, to make sure nothing will break or get tangled. The marine must then lower himself down the rope.

Marines drop from a Sea Knight helicopter to the flight deck of an amphibious assault ship during a fast-rope exercise.

The Harrier II

The AV-8B Harrier II is used by the Marine Corps for light attack or multi-role missions. As Harriers don't need a long runway, they can operate from small aircraft carriers and large amphibious assault ships, as well as on difficult **terrain** on land.

The Harrier is a V/STOL, or vertical and/or short take-off and landing, aircraft. This means it can take off using either a short ski-jump runway or straight up like a helicopter. Four nozzles direct the thrust from the engine. They can point downward for vertical take off, landing, and hovering, and then backward to propel the aircraft.

Thrust from the engines allows this Harrier to hover above the flight deck.

FACT FILE

A Marine Corps ordnance technician inspects flares loaded aboard a Harrier. Flares on military aircraft act as a defense against heat-seeking missiles. Flares need to deceive the missiles into thinking they are the aircraft, so they burn at temperatures of thousands of degrees.

With the ability to attack anywhere, the Harrier is used for missions which include attacking and destroying surface and air targets, escorting helicopters, engaging in air defense, and providing **reconnaissance**. It can fire missiles and bombs. It even has an onboard cannon.

Marine Corps pilots once carried lots of large charts in their flight bags. They are now starting to use computer tablets instead.

USS *Iwo Jima*

The USS *Iwo Jima* is an amphibious assault ship. It carries aircraft and landing craft. It supports ground forces in enemy territory and can launch an amphibious assault.

The USS *Iwo Jima*, the 24th Marine Expeditionary Unit, and two amphibious assault ships make up the *Iwo Jima* Amphibious Ready Group. The group provided disaster relief after Hurricane Katrina. The *Iwo Jima* sailed up the Mississippi River to New Orleans. It was the area's only working air field for helicopter operations during the crisis. The *Iwo Jima* has medical facilities on board, including operating theaters, wards, and x-ray facilities.

Missile launchers

The well deck can load amphibious vehicles on and off.

USS *Iwo Jima*

An amphibious assault ship is different from an aircraft carrier as its helicopters support forces ashore rather than support strike aircraft. The well deck of the *Iwo Jima* can carry three air cushion landing craft (above) and twelve mechanised landing craft (right), or 40 AAVs. The flight deck has nine helicopter landing spots.

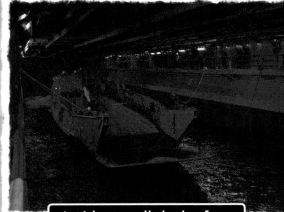

Inside a well deck of an amphibious assault ship.

FACT FILE

The USS *Iwo Jima* is named after a famous battle. During World War II, the Marine Corps played a major role in capturing the island of Iwo Jima from the Japanese. The Marine Corps War Memorial, next to Arlington National Cemetery, shows five marines and a navy corpsman raising the US flag on Iwo Jima. It was sculpted by Felix de Weldon and based on a famous photograph by Joe Rosenthal. Of the six men in the statue, three did not survive the battle.

Landing Craft

Landing craft are boats and seagoing vessels used to get infantry and vehicles from the sea to the shore during an amphibious assault.

Marines can storm the beach in their amphibious assault vehicles. Each AAV is a 26-ton (24-t) armored vehicle that carries up to 18 combat-loaded marines. It is armed with a machine gun and a grenade launcher. The AAV is the only armored vehicle in the US military that is fully capable of operations both on land and in the ocean.

FACT FILE

To be mission-ready, the Marine Corps makes sure that all of its equipment can be loaded and transported on its amphibious ships. Every piece of gear must be taken to shore by helicopter, amphibious assault vehicle, or landing craft. Careful planning is needed to fit all the tanks, trucks, aircraft, and weapons the marines will need for their missions.

A landing craft air cushion loaded with supplies launches from the well deck.

An AAV crew has a crew commander, a driver, and a rear crewman. The AAV crews to the left are doing last-minute checks while they wait in the well deck during a training exercise.

Firing Batteries

Marines in the Field Artillery don't just pull the triggers of big guns. Their job takes a lot of hard work, training, and planning. They do almost all of the things that the infantry does, but can fire **howitzers**, too.

A firing battery must drive their truck into position, leap out of the back, unhook the howitzer, and prepare to sight the gun. They quickly dig holes for the spades to dig in when the howitzer fires. They prepare an ammunition pit and a powder pit on opposite sides of the truck. The marines cover any wire and dig fighting holes. In a couple of minutes, the gun is ready to fire. Then they have to pack up their gear, hook it back up to the truck, move to another location, and start all over again.

Spades

Before the marines and artillery can move into a new position, the new area has to be scouted and prepared. A truckload of marines is sent ahead as an advance party. Once the place is secured, the marines put marking posts for the trucks to drive into position. When the trucks arrive, the set-up for firing starts all over again. Marines may do this several times in one day, and as well as sometimes at night, which can be very dangerous.

It takes several marines to load and fire a howitzer.

FACT FILE

Fighting holes are dug to give cover. They can be somewhere to sleep, too. They are dug just deep enough to lie down in. If there is time, they are dug deeper so a marine can stand and shoot. Marines dig a special side hole at the bottom called a grenade sump. If a grenade comes in, a marine can kick the grenade into the hole to absorb the blast. If there is time, they add a cover and dig a bench-like structure to sit and sleep on, away from any puddles.

Keeping Things Running

It is said marines have many roles, but one mission. All marines have a role for which they are trained, which supports the overall mission.

The Marine Corps has its own specialist support, such as aircraft and vehicle maintenance specialists. The various maintenance battalions look after and repair weapons, vehicles, aircraft, communications electronics, and general support ground equipment. Nothing would work without them.

A tank operator tightens up a new track pad on an Abrams tank. Tank operators can maintain their own tanks.

FACT FILE

A tank operator will need to know the basics to repair a tank on the move. If something really goes wrong, or it needs maintenance, a tank may be sent away to specialist turret or track mechanics.

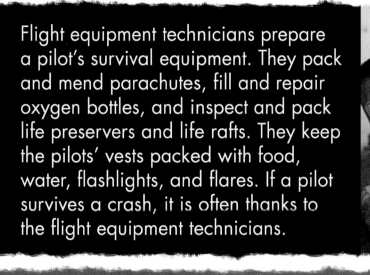

Flight equipment technicians prepare a pilot's survival equipment. They pack and mend parachutes, fill and repair oxygen bottles, and inspect and pack life preservers and life rafts. They keep the pilots' vests packed with food, water, flashlights, and flares. If a pilot survives a crash, it is often thanks to the flight equipment technicians.

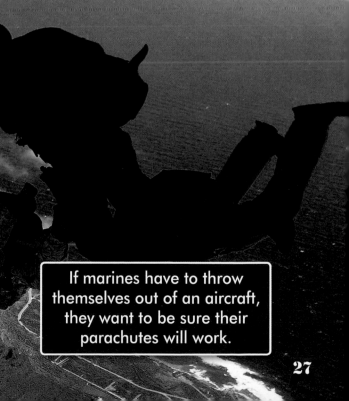

If marines have to throw themselves out of an aircraft, they want to be sure their parachutes will work.

27

Armored Vehicles

The Marine Corps has its own tanks and other armored vehicles. Tank battalions use the Abrams tank and the M88 recovery vehicle. Marines use the M1 breacher to clear pathways.

Marines' equipment is usually pretty lightweight and transportable, but not the Abrams tank. It is among the heaviest tanks in the world, but it has tremendous firepower and is surprisingly easy to maneuver. It provides armor-protected firepower to support Marine Corps ground forces.

Marines transport their tanks by landing craft, one at a time.

FACT FILE

The Marine Corps' M1 breacher is a tracked combat vehicle designed to clear pathways through minefields and clear roads of **improvised explosive devices**. The M1 is based on a tank but fitted with a front-mounted plow on metallic skis that glides along the dirt. It has mine-clearing rockets which can blow up hidden bombs at a safe distance.

The M1 is so important to the Marine Corps that it paid for its development when army funding was dropped.

The M88 recovery vehicle is used to replace damaged parts in fighting vehicles while under fire. It also moves vehicles that have become stuck. The main winch is capable of lifting an Abrams tank. The spade can be used for digging, and to anchor the vehicle to stop it tipping when using the main winch.

Winch

Spade

An M88 lifts an engine into an Abrams tank

Glossary

ammunition
(am-yuh-NIH-shun)
Objects fired from guns.

amphibious (am-FIH-bee-us)
Able to operate on land or sea.

bayoneted (BAY-oh-net-ed)
With a knife called a
bayonet attached.

cargo (KAHR-goh)
Goods transported in a ship,
airplane, or vehicle.

convoy (KON-voy)
Vehicles traveling together for
protection.

enlisted (in-LIST-ed)
Part of a military force in the
ranks below commissioned or
warrant officers.

expeditionary
(ek-spuh-DIH-shuh-ner-ee)
Having to do with military
service abroad.

grenade
(greh-NAYD)
A small bomb designed to be
thrown by hand or launched
by a rifle.

heritage (HER-uh-tij)
Something acquired from
the past.

hostile (HOS-tul)
Of or relating to an enemy.

howitzers
(HOW-it-zurs)
A short cannon capable of
firing a shell in a high arc.

improvised explosive devices
(IM-pruh-vyzd ek-SPLOH-siv dih-VY-sez)
Homemade bombs.

officer (AW-feh-sur)
A person who holds a commission in the armed forces.

reconnaissance
(ree-CON-ih-sens)
A survey, as of enemy territory, to gain information.

recruits (rih-KROOTS)
New soldiers.

restraint (rih-STRAYNT)
The act of holding someone so they cannot harm themselves or others.

terrain (tuh-RAYN)
The surface features of an area.

31

Read More

Cooke, Tim. *US Marine Corps*. Ultimate Special Forces. New York: PowerKids Press, 2013.

David, Jack. *United States Marine Corps*. Torque Books: Armed Forces. Minneapolis, MN: Bellwether Media, 2008.

Portman, Michael. *Marine Corps*. US Military Forces. New York: Gareth Stevens Publishing, 2011.

Index